Unit 3

The Heritage of Ancient Greece and Rome

Activity Book
GRADE 6

Core Knowledge Language Arts®

Copyright © 2021 Core Knowledge Foundation
www.coreknowledge.org

All Rights Reserved.

Core Knowledge®, Core Knowledge Curriculum Series™, Core Knowledge Language Arts™ and CKLA™ are trademarks of the Core Knowledge Foundation.

Trademarks and trade names are shown in this book strictly for illustrative and educational purposes and are the property of their respective owners. References herein should not be regarded as affecting the validity of said trademarks and trade names.

Printed in Canada

ISBN: 978-1-68380-650-9

Unit 3

The Heritage of Ancient Greece and Rome

Activity Book

This Activity Book contains Activity Pages that accompany the lessons from the Grade 6 CKLA Unit 3 Teacher Guide. The Activity Pages are organized and numbered according to the lesson number and the order in which they are used within the lesson. For example, if there are two Activity Pages for Lesson 4, the first will be numbered 4.1, and the second 4.2. The Activity Book is a student component, which means each student should have an Activity Book.

NAME: _____

DATE: _____

1.1 TAKE-HOME

Letter to Family

Unit 3

Our class will begin a unit in language arts in which students will read from the Core Knowledge Reader *The Heritage of Ancient Greece and Rome*. Students will read this book to learn context and background for literature such as the *Iliad,* the *Odyssey,* and Greek myths and William Shakespeare's play *The Tragedy of Julius Caesar*.

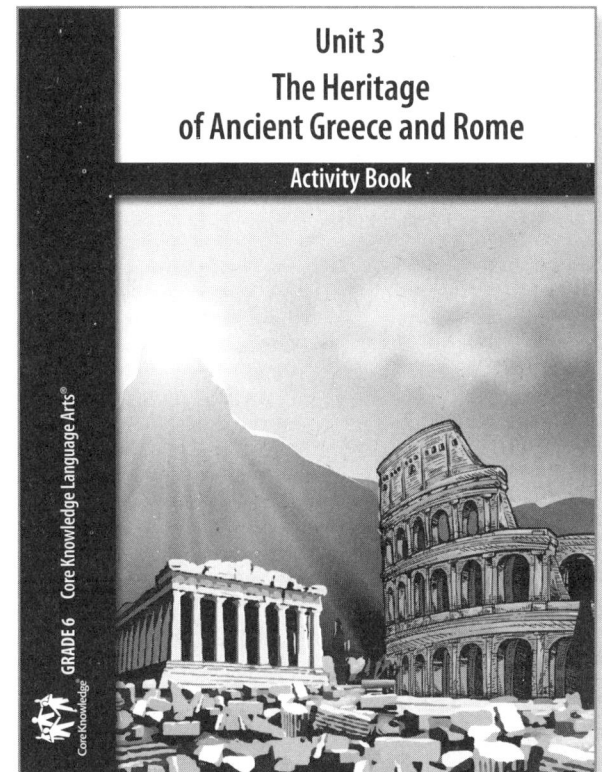

This unit gives students the opportunity to explore the influence of these two ancient civilizations on our culture today. Through various oral and written activities, students will explore specific cultural, artistic, and civic achievements of ancient Greek and Roman society and the impact of these societies on modern society and our everyday lives.

You are invited to share and explore the reading and activities in this unit with your child. Students may have several homework assignments in which they may ask you or other family members about terms and ideas that are key to the understanding of these early civilizations' influence on our own culture.

If you have any questions of concerns, please do not hesitate to contact me.

NAME: _____

DATE: _____

1.2 ACTIVITY PAGE

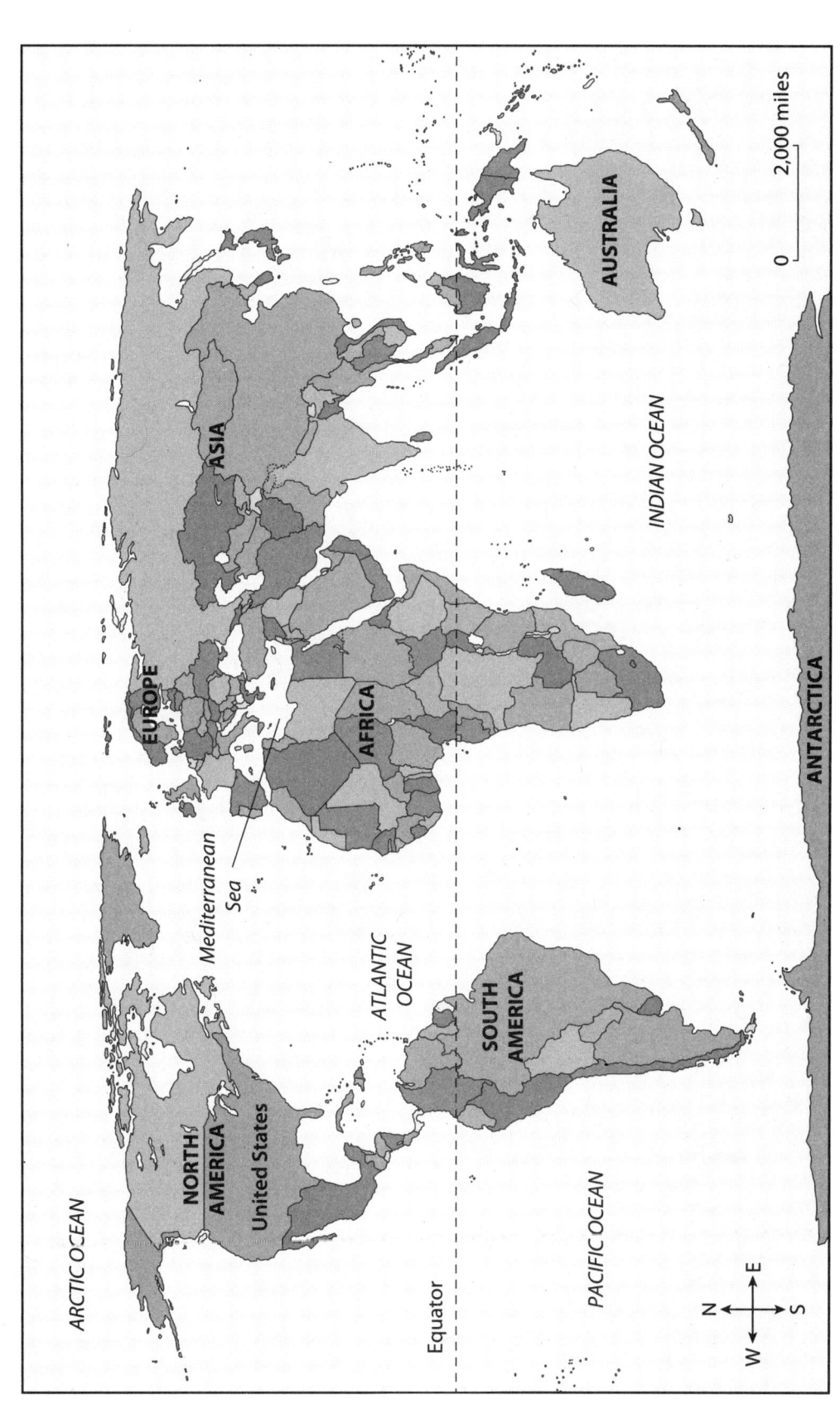

NAME:

DATE:

1.3 ACTIVITY PAGE

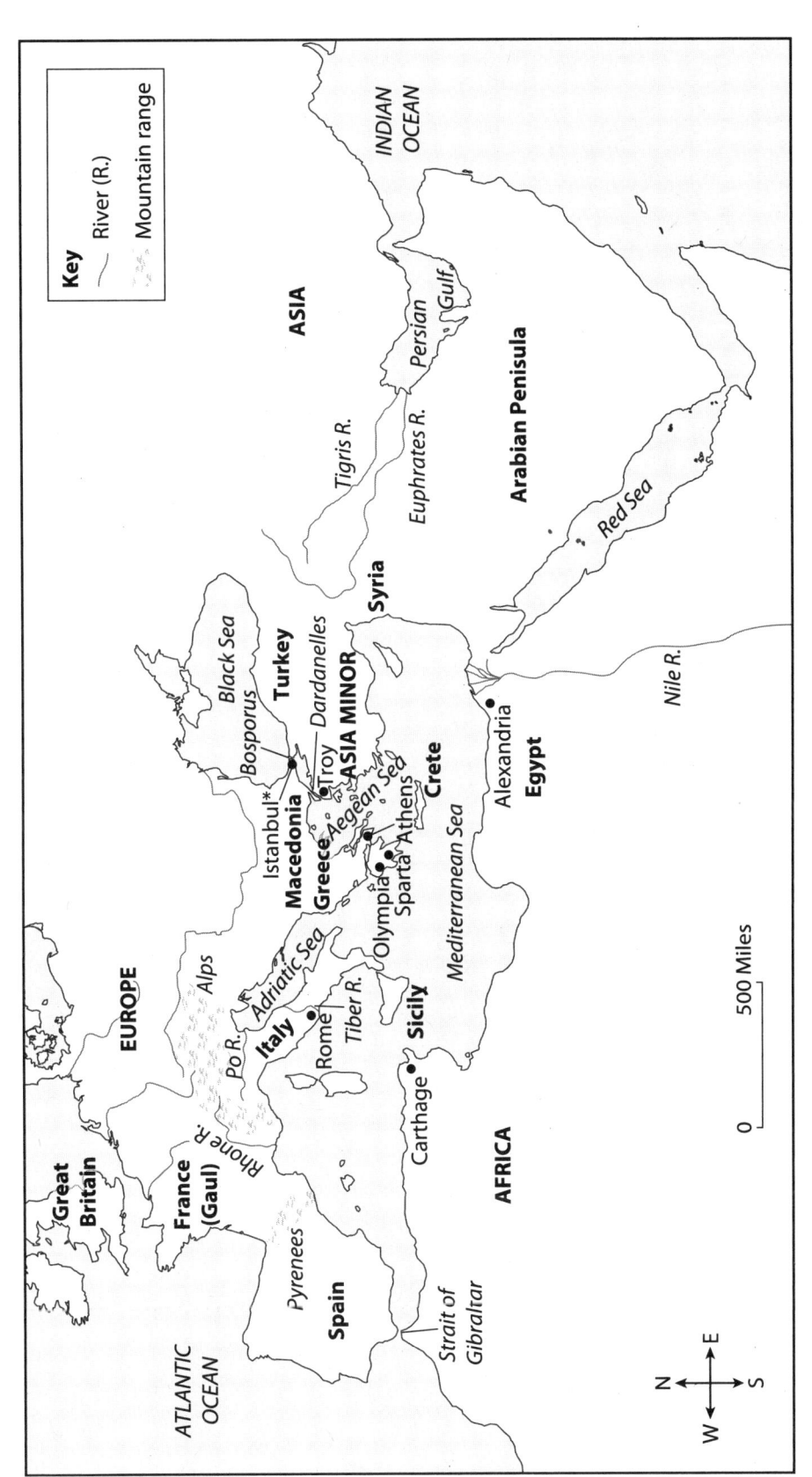

Map of the Mediterranean Region

*Note: Modern-day Istanbul was known as Byzantium and Constantinople during ancient Greek and Roman times.

NAME:

DATE:

Vocabulary for "The Heritage of Greece and Rome"

1. **civilization,** *n.* a society, or group of people, with similar religious beliefs, customs, language, and government (**civilizations**) (2)

2. **influence,** *v.* to have an effect on (**influenced**) (2)

3. **architecture,** *n.* the art of designing and constructing buildings (3)

4. **inherit,** *v.* to receive something from a former owner or someone who came before (**inherited**) (7)

NAME: _____

DATE: _____

1.5 ACTIVITY PAGE

Vocabulary for "The Ancient Greek City-States"

1. **misleading,** *adj.* tending to cause people to believe the wrong thing (**8**)

2. **unified,** *adj.* whole, united, acting as one (**8**)

3. **fresco,** *n.* a watercolor painting on plaster (**9**)

4. **frieze,** *n.* a wide, sculpted wall decoration (**10**)

5. **groundbreaking,** *adj.* never done before (**11**)

6. **unity,** *n.* the state of being whole or in agreement (**13**)

NAME:
DATE:

Vocabulary for "Athens"

1. **debate,** *v.* to formally discuss or argue multiple views about a topic (**14**)

2. **proposal,** *n.* an idea or plan put forward for discussion with others (**14**)

3. **council,** *n.* a group of people who meet regularly to make decisions (**16**)

4. **term,** *n.* a set amount of time that a person spends in a certain position in a government (**16**)

5. **bribery,** *n.* the act of giving money or something of value to illegally influence a person in power (**17**)

NAME:

DATE:

Vocabulary for "Sparta"

1. **emphasize,** *v.* to stress strongly, give special importance to (**emphasized**) (**22**)

2. **disciplined**, *adj.* self-controlled (**26**)

3. **extravagant,** *adj.* more than necessary, excessive (**27**)

4. **biased,** *adj.* unfair toward a person, group, or viewpoint (**27**)

5. **hostile**, *adj.* unfriendly toward someone or something, in opposition to (**28**)

6. **excel,** *v.* to be very good at knowing or doing something (**29**)

7. **rivalry,** *n.* a competition between groups for the same goals (**29**)

8. **fateful,** *adj.* having significant and negative results (**29**)

NAME: _____

DATE: _____

2.3 ACTIVITY PAGE

"Sparta"

As you read "Sparta," answer these questions.

1. What does the author compare and contrast in the first paragraph? (Page 22)

   _____

2. How many years of military training did Sparta require? (Page 22)

   _____

3. What text feature does the author use with the image on page 23?

   _____

4. What text structure does the author use to describe the military training of Spartan males? (Page 24)

   _____

5. How did Spartan women contribute to Sparta's military culture? (Page 24)

   _____

   _____

6. Who were the helots? (Page 25)

   _____

   _____

7. What text features appear on page 26?

   _____

   _____

Core Knowledge Language Arts | Grade 6

8. What does the heading "Contrasting Lifestyles" hint about the text structure that follows? (Page 27)

9. Why did the Spartan elders permit Spartan soldiers to dance? (Page 27)

10. Which city-state (Athens or Sparta) do you think had a culture most like ours? Why?

NAME: _____

DATE: _____

3.1 ACTIVITY PAGE

Identifying an Author's Viewpoint (Opinion)

Fill in the chart with the author's opinion about "The Golden Age of Athens." Then record three examples of text evidence that support this opinion.

Author's Opinion	Text Evidence
	Example 1:
	Example 2:
	Example 3:

Now write an opinion of your own. Be sure to support it with an example from the text.

My Opinion	Text Evidence

NAME:

DATE:

Vocabulary for "The Golden Age of Athens"

1. **alliance,** *n.* a group of city-states (or countries or people) who agree to help one another (**32**)

2. **influential,** *adj.* having a great deal of control (**32**)

3. **victorious,** *adj.* having won a fight or battle (**33**)

4. **campaign,** *n.* a military operation intended to achieve a particular objective (**campaigns**) (**33**)

5. **complex,** *n.* a group of similar buildings (**34**); *adj.* having many connected parts (**38**)

6. **recruit,** *v.* to obtain the services of (**recruited**) (**36**)

7. **contemporary,** *adj.* existing at the same time (**39**)

8. **urn,** *n.* a ceramic vase that has a base (**urns**) (**40**)

9. **rite,** *n.* a ceremony, usually religious (**rites**) (**40**)

10. **raucous,** *adj.* wild and noisy (**41**)

NAME: _____
DATE: _____

3.3 ACTIVITY PAGE

Punctuation in Compound Sentences

Complete each compound sentence as indicated, using a semicolon or a comma followed by the conjunction in parentheses.

1. (**but**) Sofia doesn't enjoy soft drinks, but she likes orange juice.

2. (**;**) Shelby missed her favorite show last night _____.

3. (**or**) I need to find a new wheel for my bike _____.

4. (**;**) Martin loves to exercise _____.

5. (**and**) My cousin's dog ran away _____.

6. (**but**) The class wasn't interested in taking a field trip _____.

7. (**but**) Give me a call tonight _____.

8. (;) I read that Kansas is located in the center of the country _____

_____.

9. (and) We all heard the explosion _____

_____.

10. (or) Should we go ahead and leave now _____

_____?

NAME: _____
DATE: _____

3.3 CONTINUED — TAKE-HOME

Practice Punctuation in Compound Sentences

Examine each compound sentence. If it is written correctly, write "correct" on the line that follows. If it is not, rewrite the sentence correctly.

1. Christine likes to dance, and she does so whenever she can.

   _____

   _____

   _____

2. Janine is very smart, she is writing a novel.

   _____

   _____

   _____

3. The soldier slept for sixteen hours; it had been a long day.

   _____

   _____

   _____

4. I'm looking forward to going but I need to borrow some money.

   _____

   _____

   _____

5. Arjun could spend the weekend at Cam's house he also could stay home.

6. The girls chased the rabbit; but they did not catch it.

7. Should I stay, or should I go?

8. My brother went home early but, I stayed for another hour.

NAME: _____

DATE: _____

3.4 | ACTIVITY PAGE

Research Topic and Question

You may research a person, place, or event. Circle up to five topics that interest you. You may also add related topics of your own.

Person	Place	Event
Alexander the Great	Temple of Olympian Zeus	Trojan War
Archimedes	Parthenon	Olympic Games
Aristotle	Temple of Hera	Coin currency established
Pericles	City-state of Athens	Second Peloponnesian War
Plato	City-state of Sparta	Battle of Issus
Socrates	Great Theater of Epidaurus	Roman invasion of Greece

Write a research question about your topic. Begin your question with What, Why or How.

_____

_____

_____

_____

_____

_____

NAME: _____

DATE: _____

4.1 ACTIVITY PAGE

Vocabulary for "Greek Philosophy and Socrates"

1. **adversity,** *n.* hardship or misfortune (**42**)

2. **urgency,** *n.* a state of extreme importance (**42**)

3. **contradiction,** *n.* the state when two things oppose one another (**contradictions**) (**45**)

4. **excerpt,** *n.* a short piece from a larger body of work (**45**)

5. **shortcoming,** *n.* a fault in someone's personality or character (**shortcomings**) (**47**)

6. **mislead,** *v.* to purposefully cause someone to form a wrong idea (**misled**) (**47**)

7. **hemlock,** *n.* a highly poisonous plant (**49**)

NAME: _____
DATE: _____

4.2 ACTIVITY PAGE

"Greek Philosophy and Socrates"

As you read "Greek Philosophy and Socrates," answer these questions.

1. What connection does the text make between the Peloponnesian War and the blossoming of philosophy in Greece? (Page 44)

   _____

   _____

2. What replaced myths as the method the Greeks used to examine life? (Page 44)

   _____

   _____

3. What does the word *soul* refer to? (Page 45)

   _____

   _____

4. How did Socrates differ from earlier Greek philosophers? (Page 46)

   _____

   _____

5. Why did Socrates ask people questions? (Page 47)

   _____

   _____

   _____

6. What was a sophist? (Page 48)

   _____

   _____

7. Who wrote about the death of Socrates? (Page 50)

   _____

   _____

8. Why was Socrates executed? (Page 49)

   _____

   _____

NAME: _____
DATE: _____

4.3 TAKE-HOME

Greek and Latin Roots *ante, astron, bios, ge*

Fill in this chart with the origin and meaning of each root.

ROOT	ORIGIN	MEANING
ante		
astron		
bios		
ge		

Write a definition for each using a meaning from the chart above. You can check the meaning of your definitions in a dictionary.

WORD	DEFINITION
ante meridiem	
astronomer	
biology	
antebellum	
geography	
biography	
geocentric	
anterior	
astronaut	

NAME: _____
DATE: _____

4.3 CONTINUED — TAKE-HOME

Greek and Latin Roots *ante, astron, bios, ge*

Use your knowledge of the roots you've learned to match each term with its definition.

1. _____ ante meridiem   A. before noon
2. _____ antebellum   B. someone who studies the stars
3. _____ anticipate   C. the study of physical life
4. _____ antique   D. before a war
5. _____ astronaut   E. the study of Earth's features
6. _____ astronomer   F. a written account of someone's life
7. _____ biography   G. to look forward to or to prepare for something before it happens
8. _____ biology   H. with Earth in the center
9. _____ geocentric   I. from a time before the present
10. _____ geography   J. someone who travels among the stars

NAME: _____

DATE: _____

4.4 ACTIVITY PAGE

Answer the Research Question with Sources

Record the answers to your research question and the sources where you found your answers.

Research Question:		
Answer	**Source**	**Additional Questions**

NAME: _____
DATE: _____

5.1 ACTIVITY PAGE

Outline

Introduction (paragraph 1): An action, dialogue, or thought that will get readers interested in reading my essay: _____

_____

One-sentence explanation of my research question: _____

_____

Answer #1 (paragraph 2): _____

_____

Ways in which this answer ties to my question: _____

_____

Answer #2 (paragraph 3): _____

_____

Ways in which this answer ties to my question: _____

_____

Answer #3 (paragraph 4): _____

_____

Ways in which this answer ties to my question: _____

_____

NAME: _____

DATE: _____

5.2 ACTIVITY PAGE

Summarize or Paraphrase Sources

Source Says:

"While in Macedonia [Aristotle] tutored the king of Macedonia's son … [who] would later become a famous conqueror … known as Alexander the Great."

Editors of Britannica Kids. (n.d.). "Aristotle." Retrieved December 11, 2020, from https://kids.britannica.com/kids/article/Aristotle/352779

Summary

Aristotle tutored the prince of Macedonia, who would later be known as Alexander the Great.

Paraphrase

In Macedonia, Aristotle tutored the king's son, who would later become the well-known conqueror Alexander the Great.

Now, you try …

Source Says:

"Aristotle laid the foundation for most modern sciences. He thought that people should observe nature and gain knowledge from their senses."

Summary:

_____

_____

_____

_____

Paraphrase:

NAME: _____
DATE: _____

5.3 ACTIVITY PAGE

Quote from Sources

Source Says:

"Aristotle's writings on ethics (what is right and wrong) and politics still fascinate modern readers."

Editors of Britannica Kids. (n.d.). "Aristotle." Retrieved December 11, 2020, from https://kids.britannica.com/kids/article/Aristotle/352779

Embedded Quotation:

Even today, the thinking of Aristotle influences "ethics (what is right and wrong) and politics" (Britannica "Aristotle").

Now, you try …

Source Says:

"During the Middle Ages, scholars in Western Europe studied Aristotle through the work of ancient Roman and Arab scholars."

Embedded Quotation:

_____

_____

_____

_____

_____

_____

Core Knowledge Language Arts | Grade 6   Activity Book | Unit 3   41

NAME: _____

DATE: _____

6.1 ACTIVITY PAGE

Vocabulary for "Alexander and the Hellenistic Period"

1. **disorganized,** a*dj.* not under sufficient control **(54)**

2. **stronghold,** *n.* a strong, secure shelter **(56)**)

3. **extraordinary,** *adj.* unusual and amazing **(58)**

4. **successor,** *n.* a person or thing that follows another person or thing **(59)**

5. **papyrus,** *n.* in ancient times, a material used to write on **(61)**

NAME: _____

DATE: _____

6.2 TAKE-HOME

Punctuation with Nonrestrictive Clauses

Complete these two sentences to describe the difference between a restrictive clause and a nonrestrictive clause.

1. A _____ clause contributes necessary information to a sentence.

2. A _____ clause contributes information to a sentence, but it can be removed without changing the sentence's meaning.

Read each sentence. Determine whether the underlined clause is restrictive or nonrestrictive. Write the type on the line. If the clause is nonrestrictive, rewrite the sentence using correct commas, dashes, or parentheses. Use each type of punctuation at least once.

1. Cynthia who is from California just bought a car.

   _____

   _____

2. Michael who plays basketball did not join the drama club.

   _____

   _____

3. The woman who drives our school bus got married last week.

   _____

   _____

4. Apples <u>which come in many varieties</u> are my favorite fruit.

   _____

   _____

5. The store <u>at which Mrs. Anders works</u> is closed on Tuesdays.

   _____

   _____

6. The movie <u>that I want to see</u> is playing at eight o'clock.

   _____

   _____

NAME: _____

DATE: _____

6.2 CONTINUED | TAKE-HOME

Practice Punctuation with Nonrestrictive Clauses

Examine each pair of sentences, and place an "X" after the one that is punctuated correctly.

1. My dad who is wearing the blue coat is waiting for the bus. _____

    My dad, who is wearing the blue coat, is waiting for the bus. _____

2. The car that I got for my birthday already needs repairs. _____

    The car, that I got for my birthday, already needs repairs. _____

3. I want to tell our coach whose name is Duane Murdock that I appreciate his efforts. _____

    I want to tell our coach, whose name is Duane Murdock, that I appreciate his efforts. _____

4. Marcia had to eat fast food, which was all she could afford. _____

    Marcia had to eat, fast food which was all she could afford. _____

5. Denver which is where my parents were born, is the largest city in Colorado. _____

    Denver, which is the largest city in Colorado, is where my parents were born. _____

6. The book, which took me a month to find, was worth the wait. _____

    The book which took me a month to find was worth the wait. _____

NAME:

DATE:

6.3 ACTIVITY PAGE

Concluding Statement

Read the sample concluding statement below.

The story of Aristotle shows the spread of Western thinking throughout the world. His ideas were studied and adopted in Europe, the Middle East, and North Africa. His influence is evident in fields such as science, logic, persuasion, and the arts. Yet his most important legacy may be that of the forever student. He spent his life studying, writing, and teaching so that the world might be better organized and understood.

Choose a sentence starter to begin your own concluding statement. Circle the sentence starter that you will use. Then, draft your concluding statement in your Writing Journal.

The story of _____ shows that _____.

This information has shown that _____.

These facts may have convinced you that _____.

The overall conclusion is that _____.

The study concludes _____.

Toward this end _____.

After all has been said _____.

For this reason _____.

As a result _____.

To sum up _____.

NAME: _____
DATE: _____

Vocabulary for "The Roman Republic"

1. **legend,** *n.* a story that has been handed down from person to person over a long period of time; the story may or may not be true **(62)**

2. **found,** *v.* to establish or build **(founded) (62)**

3. **modest,** *adj.* small or limited **(63)**

4. **revolt,** *n.* an attempt to put an end to a ruling power **(64)**

5. **distinction,** *n.* category or grouping **(66)**

6. **station,** *v.* to place someone or something, especially military, in a certain place **(stationed) (67)**

7. **career,** *n.* a job **(69)**

8. **ambitious,** *adj.* wanting to succeed **(69)**

NAME: _____
DATE: _____

7.2 ACTIVITY PAGE

"The Roman Republic"

As you read "The Roman Republic," answer these questions.

1. Who were Romulus and Remus? (Page 62)

   _____
   _____
   _____

2. How do most historians believe Rome was actually first formed? (Page 64)

   _____
   _____
   _____

3. How did plebians differ from patricians? (Page 65)

   _____
   _____
   _____

4. What resulted from the tension between plebians and patricians? (Page 65)

   _____
   _____
   _____

5. What kind of government eventually developed in the Roman Republic? (Page 66)

6. How did the Roman Republic organize and rule the lands it conquered? (Page 67)

7. How did the Roman Republic often treat those it conquered? (Page 68)

8. What problem arose as the Roman army assumed greater power? (Page 69)

NAME: _____

DATE: _____

7.3 ACTIVITY PAGE

Greek and Latin Affixes *mega–, mini–, micro–, –en*

Review the information on these two charts.

PREFIX	MEANING	AFFIXED WORD	MEANING
mega–	large or great	Megalopolis	a large city in ancient Greece
mini–	small or smaller	minimize	make smaller
micro–	small or smaller	microcomputer	a small computer

SUFFIX	MEANING	AFFIXED WORD	MEANING
–en	made of (adjective) to make or become (verb)	golden weaken	made of gold to become weaker

Write a definition for each using the chart above and checking your meaning in a dictionary.

WORD	DEFINITION
megalomaniac	
enliven	
megalith	
sharpen	
miniseries	

earthen	
microchip	
straighten	
minicam	
microsurgery	

NAME:

DATE:

Works Cited

Book

Author. Britannica Kids. date. sponsoring organization. Retrieved June 29, 2021. https://kids.britannica.com/kids/article/Aristotle/352779
Last name, First name. *Title.* Place of publication: Publisher, Copyright date.

Sáenz, Benjamin Alire. *Aristotle and Dante Discover the Secrets of the Universe.* New York: Simon and Schuster, 2012.

Article

Last name, First name. "Title of Article." *Publication name.* Date: pages.

Byrne, Lucy Sweeney. "Poetics by Aristotle: An Essential Read." *The Irish Times.* November 2020: B2–B3.

Website

Title of Website, "Title of Article," date accessed, URL link.

Britannica Kids, "Aristotle," accessed June 29, 2021, https://kids.britannica.com/kids/article/Aristotle/352779.

NAME: _____
DATE: _____

8.1 ACTIVITY PAGE

Vocabulary for "Julius Caesar: A Great Roman"

1. **professional**, *adj.* done as a career or profession (**70**)

2. **status**, *n.* position in society (**72**)

3. **charming**, *adj.* pleasant, attractive, likable (**72**)

4. **arrogant**, *adj.* having a pushy, snobbish attitude (**73**)

5. **public figure**, *n.* someone the public in general knows about (**76**)

6. **tirelessly**, *adv.* with a lot of effort and energy (**76**)

7. **convulsion**, *n.* a violent, unwilling muscle contraction (**77**)

8. **chaos**, *n.* a state of complete confusion (**77**)

9. **betrayal**, *n.* the act of violating a friendship (**78**)

NAME: _____

DATE: _____

8.2 TAKE-HOME

Small-Group Questions: "Julius Caesar: A Great Roman"

1. What career did Julius Caesar choose as a way to better himself?

   _____

2. In what ways had the Roman government and army changed by Caesar's time?

   _____

   _____

   _____

3. What was Caesar's plan for gaining power?

   _____

   _____

4. How and when did Caesar become part of the Roman government?

   _____

   _____

5. What decision faced Caesar when he was invited to Rome to become consul the second time?

   _____

   _____

6. What happened as a result of the conflict sparked by Caesar's return to Rome?

7. Hiw did Caesar's actions support the idea that he wanted to be a great leader?

8. What action of Caesar's most likely led to his assassination?

9. Who led the assassination plot against Caesar, and how many members of the Senate were involved in the plot?

10. What happened to Caesar and Rome about a month after he was made dictator for life?

NAME: _____
DATE: _____

8.3 ACTIVITY PAGE

Spelling Words

Write the correct word to complete each sentence. Words will not be used more than once; some words will not be used.

dependent	gymnasium	Britain
possess	biographer	weaken
astronomy	microbiology	ante meridiem
geography	golden	Megalopolis
peasant	minimum	miniature

1. The runners felt themselves _____ as the afternoon grew warmer.

2. The terms *England* and _____ are often confused.

3. The Latin phrase _____ is where we get our abbreviation for "morning."

4. He had grown _____ on her company and did not want her to leave.

5. The class went to a planetarium, where they learned about _____.

6. Cameron wanted to learn about different countries, so he bought a _____ book.

7. Robert Caro is a famous _____ who wrote about former president Lyndon Johnson.

8. Farmers know that when wheat turns _____, it is ready to harvest.

9. Everybody said that Shanice was a _____ version of her mother.

10. There was a town in Greece called _____, a word that means "very large city."

Write sentences using spelling words of your choice that were not used in the first ten sentences. Be sure to use correct capitalization and punctuation.

11. _____

_____

_____

_____

_____

_____

12 _____

_____

_____

_____

_____

_____

NAME: _____

DATE: _____

8.4 ACTIVITY PAGE

Research Essay Rubric

	Exemplary	Strong	Developing	Beginning
Introduction	Includes an engaging introductory statement to get readers interested in the topic.	Includes an introductory statement that is linked to the topic.	Introductory statement is included but may be unclear or not clearly linked to the topic.	Does not include an introductory statement to get readers interested in the topic.
	Research question is clearly presented.	Research question is presented.	Research question is presented but may be unclear.	Research question is not presented.
Body	Body includes 3–4 paragraphs that present information from two or more sources that answers the research question; transitions between paragraphs are clear and effective.	Body includes 3–4 paragraphs that present information from two sources that answers the research question; uses adequate transitions.	Body includes information from 1–2 sources that attempts to answer the research question; paragraphs and transitions may be unclear.	Body may present inadequate information or information not related to the topic; little attempt to use paragraph structure.

	Exemplary	Strong	Developing	Beginning
Conclusion	Essay conclusion effectively summarizes content and answers research question.	Essay conclusion acceptably summarizes content and answers research question.	Essay conclusion insufficiently summarizes content and answers research question.	Essay conclusion fails to summarize content or address research question.
Research	Quoting and paraphrasing are used effectively to communicate information and avoid plagiarism; includes a complete and accurate works cited page of all sources.	Quoting and paraphrasing are used to avoid plagiarism; includes a works cited page of all sources with few or no errors.	Quoting or paraphrasing are used but includes errors or occasionally copies from the source text without quoting; works cited page may be incomplete or have significant errors.	Quoting or paraphrasing are minimally used; sentences and phrases are copied directly from the source text; works cited page is missing or has significant errors.

You may correct capitalization, punctuation, and grammar errors while you are revising. However, if you create a final copy of your writing to publish, you will use an editing checklist to address those types of mistakes after you revise.

NAME: _____

DATE: _____

8.5 ACTIVITY PAGE

Peer Review Checklist for Research Essay

Complete this checklist as you read the draft of the research essay written by a classmate.
Y = yes   N = no   SW = somewhat

Author's Name: _____   Reviewer's Name: _____

_____ The research essay includes a clear introduction that introduces the research question.

_____ The research essay includes three or four paragraphs that answer the research question.

_____ The research essay uses information from at least two sources.

_____ The research essay uses quotes and paraphrasing to avoid plagiarizing research sources.

_____ The research essay includes a works cited page that properly cites all sources.

_____ The research essay has a conclusion that sums up the research.

_____ The research essay uses a consistent formal style throughout.

Ways in Which Your Research Essay Meets the Requirements of the Assignment	Ways in Which You Can Better Meet the Requirements of the Assignment

NAME: _____

DATE: _____

9.1 ACTIVITY PAGE

Vocabulary for "The Fall of the Roman Empire"

1. **wrong,** *n.* an illegal action (**wrongs**) (**80**)

2. **prosperity,** *n.* the state of being materially successful (**80**)

3. **declare,** *v.* to state something as a truth (**declaring**) (**82**)

4. **adequate,** *adj.* enough to meet a need (**85**)

5. **barbarian,** *n.* a person, often foreign, considered inferior and violent (**barbarians**) (**85**)

6. **grandeur,** *n.* the state of being remarkable, very impressive, or special (**88**)

NAME:

DATE:

Causes of the Fall of Rome

As you read each section, note reasons why Rome was weakened and eventually collapsed.

Strengths and Weaknesses

_____

_____

_____

_____

Money Troubles

_____

_____

_____

_____

Gap between Rich and Poor

_____

_____

_____

_____

Government Officials and Armies

_____

_____

_____

The Germanic Tribes

_____

_____

_____

Goths and Vandals

_____

_____

_____

The Rise of Islam

_____

_____

_____

Practice Prefixes *mega–*, *mini–*, *micro–* and Suffix *–en*

Use your knowledge of the prefixes and suffixes to match each term with its definition.

1. _____ earthen   A. one who thinks oneself great

2. _____ enliven   B. to make livelier

3. _____ megalith   C. a large stone monument

4. _____ megalomaniac   D. to become sharper

5. _____ microchip   E. a short television series

6. _____ microsurgery   F. made of dirt

7. _____ minicam   G. a tiny wafer that holds circuitry

8. _____ miniseries   H. to become straighter

9. _____ sharpen   I. a small camera

10. _____ straighten   J. surgery done with very small instruments

NAME: _____
DATE: _____

9.4 ACTIVITY PAGE

Practice Spelling Words

Complete a sentence for each of the spelling words. Each sentence should show the meaning of the underlined spelling word.

1. The biographer wrote _____
   _____

2. Astronomy is _____
   _____

3. Geography is _____
   _____

4. Microbiology is _____
   _____

5. The miniature house _____
   _____

6. We go to the gymnasium to _____
   _____

7. If you possess something, you _____
   _____

Core Knowledge Language Arts | Grade 6   Activity Book | Unit 3

8. A peasant was someone _____

_____

9. If you are dependent on something, you _____

_____

10. Megalopolis was _____

_____

11. Britain is _____

_____

12. An example of something that is golden is _____

_____

13. If you ask for the minimum of something, you want _____

_____

14. To weaken something means to _____

_____

15. If you woke up in the ante meridiem, you _____

_____

NAME: _____
DATE: _____

9.5 ACTIVITY PAGE

Research Essay Editing Checklist

Research Essay Editing Checklist	After reviewing for each type of edit, place a check mark here.
Vocabulary	
• I have used academic and domain-specific vocabulary correctly. • I have provided my readers with context clues to help them understand the meaning of potentially unfamiliar language.	
Format	
• I have titled my writing. • I have included the proper heading, including my name, my teacher's name, the class title, and the date. • My essay answers a research question using sources. • Each paragraph focuses on a part of the answer to my research question. • I have made sure to paraphrase, summarize, and use quotations in order to avoid plagiarism. • I have used in-text notations and a works cited page to cite sources.	

Research Essay Editing Checklist	After reviewing for each type of edit, place a check mark here.
Grammar	
• I have checked my work to make sure I have used correct grammar.	
Spelling	
• I have checked my work for spelling errors. • I have correctly spelled words with the roots *ante*, *astron*, *bios*, *ge*, *mega*, *mikros*, and *minus*. • I have correctly spelled words with the prefixes *mega–*, *mini–*, *micro–* and the suffix *–en*.	
Punctuation	
• I have punctuated simple, compound, and complex sentences correctly. • I have correctly used semicolons/commas with *and, but,* or *or* in compound sentences. • I have used commas, parentheses, or dashes to set off nonrestrictive/parenthetical elements.	

NAME: _____
DATE: _____

10.1 ACTIVITY PAGE

Speaking and Listening Rubric

	Exemplary	Strong	Developing	Beginning
Speaking	Claims and findings are clearly stated.	Claims and findings are stated.	Claims and findings are stated but unclear.	Claims and findings are not stated.
	Ideas are effectively sequenced.	Ideas are partially sequenced.	Ideas are vaguely sequenced.	Ideas are not sequenced.
	Descriptions, facts, and details are effectively presented to support main ideas and themes.	Descriptions, facts, and details are presented with some effectiveness in supporting main ideas and themes.	Descriptions, facts, and details are presented with little effectiveness in supporting main ideas and themes.	Descriptions, facts, and details are not presented.
	Content is presented with exemplary eye contact, adequate volume, and consistently clear pronunciation.	Content is presented with an adequate level of eye contact and volume and mostly clear pronunciation.	Content is presented with poor eye contact and inadequate volume and pronunciation.	Content is presented with no appreciable eye contact and poor volume and pronunciation.

	Exemplary	Strong	Developing	Beginning
Listening	Audience consistently listens attentively, asks relevant questions, waits for others to finish before speaking, and allows others to speak.	Audience mostly listens attentively, asks relevant questions, waits for others to finish before speaking, and allows others to speak.	Audience intermittently listens, asks few relevant questions, and is mostly inattentive to fellow students.	Audience pays little or no attention, asks no questions, and does not interact with fellow students.

NAME: _____

DATE: _____

Spelling Assessment

Write the spelling words as your teacher calls them out.

1. _____

2. _____

3. _____

4. _____

5. _____

6. _____

7. _____

8. _____

9. _____

10. _____

11. _____

12. _____

13. _____

14. _____

15. _____

NAME: _____

DATE: _____

11.1 ASSESSMENT

Unit Assessment—*The Heritage of Ancient Greece and Rome*

Today you will read two selections. After reading the first selection, you will answer several questions based on it. Then, you will read the second selection and answer several questions based on it. Some of the questions have two parts. You should answer Part A of the question before you answer Part B.

"The First Persian War"

The Beginning of the War

1. In the first chapter, you learned that there were a number of Greek city-states on the coast of Asia Minor. About 546 BCE, these city-states came under the control of the Persians, who appointed harsh tyrants to rule each of them.

2. Around 499 BCE, the city-state of Miletus (/mye*lee*tus/) rebelled against Persian rule. The people of Miletus asked the Greeks in other city-states to help them overthrow the Persians. The Spartans refused, but the Athenians agreed to help.

3. In 498 BCE, the Athenians crossed the Aegean Sea to Asia Minor. They conquered the Persian-controlled city of Sardis. When the other Greek city-states in Asia Minor learned of Athens's victory, they decided to join the revolt against the Persians. The Athenians felt their point had been made, and they went home. Within three years, the Persian king Darius had put down the revolt and regained control of the Greek city-states in Asia Minor.

4. Even though they had regained control of their empire, the Persians were angry with the Athenians. In 490 BCE, the Persians crossed the Aegean Sea to punish the Athenians.

Marathon

5. The Athenians met the Persians on the plain at Marathon, about twenty-six miles from Athens. The Athenians were badly outnumbered, but they decided to attack. The Greek charge was a success. The Persians broke ranks and fled to their ships, and the Greeks cut them down as they ran. By the end of the battle, more than six thousand Persians were dead, while only 192 Greeks had fallen.

6. According to legend, the Greeks ordered a messenger to run to Athens and deliver news of the victory. The messenger ran the twenty-six miles to Athens, gasped out his victory announcement, "Rejoice, we conquer!", and died of exhaustion. Today, we use the word *marathon* to refer to a 26.2-mile footrace.

7. Marathon was an extremely important battle. Because the Athenians won, they were filled with self-confidence. They began to think that they were the most powerful of all the Greeks.

Thermopylae

8. The Persians were not yet done with the Athenians, however. In 480 BCE, another Persian army was sent to defeat the Greeks. With an army of more than one hundred thousand men, as well as six hundred to seven hundred ships, the Persian king Xerxes (/zurk*seez/) (486–465 BCE) was determined to conquer all of Greece.

9. Athens and Sparta put aside their disagreements and united against the Persians. They were joined by a few other city-states. The Greeks had between two hundred and three hundred ships and an army of ten thousand men. The army was led by King Leonidas (/lee*ahn*ee*dus/) of Sparta.

10. The Greeks realized that the longer they could put off a major battle, the better their chances would be. The Greeks decided to delay the Persian army by engaging them at a place called Thermopylae (/thur*mahp*uh*lee/), about seventy-five miles northwest of Athens. Thermopylae was a narrow **pass** between high cliffs and the sea. Because of the narrowness of the pass, the Greeks hoped that the Persians would be unable to use their entire army and therefore the Greeks might be able to hold the pass.

11. Things did not turn out exactly as planned. Leonidas and his troops showed great courage and managed to hold the pass for two days, but a native of the area, a man by the name of Ephialtes (/eff*ee*awl*teez/), showed the Persians how to use a mountain path to slip around the Greeks. When Leonidas realized what had happened, he ordered the majority of the Greeks to retreat. He and three hundred Spartans stayed behind to hold back the Persian army. All three hundred Spartans died defending the pass.

NAME: _____

DATE: _____

11.1 CONTINUED ASSESSMENT

Questions

1. Which sentence is the best description of this text?

   A. It is a primary source written by an ancient Greek historian.

   B. It is a primary source based on documents and artifacts of the period.

   C. It is a secondary source based on historical research and scholarship.

   D. It is a secondary source written by scholars who studied original Greek drama.

2. What sparked the first Persian War?

   _____

   _____

   _____

   _____

   _____

3. Which of these correctly describes the 490 BCE battle between the Athenians and Persians on the plain at Marathon?

   A. Although the Athenians were greatly outnumbered, they won.

   B. Although the Persians were greatly outnumbered, they won.

   C. The battle resulted in the withdrawal of the Persians from Asia Minor.

   D. The battle resulted in a truce between the Persians and Athenians.

4. What do you think prompted Athens and Sparta to set aside their rivalry? Use evidence from the text to support your reasoning.

_____

_____

_____

_____

5. PART A: Which side does the author portray more positively, Persia or Greece?

_____

PART B: What evidence from the text supports your answer in Part A?

_____

_____

_____

NAME: _____

DATE: _____

11.1 CONTINUED — ASSESSMENT

"Ancient Greece's Third Great Philosopher"

Aristotle

1. Just as Socrates found a great student in Plato, so Plato found a great student in Aristotle. Aristotle was born around 384 BCE in Macedonia, a country north of Greece. There, his father had been a doctor in the court of the king, Amyntas III. When Aristotle came to Athens, he studied with Plato and stayed at Plato's school for twenty years before starting his own school, called the Lyceum (/lye*see*um/).

2. Aristotle was greatly influenced both by his father and by Plato. His father had influenced him because, in ancient times, knowledge and skills were passed from father to son. Aristotle's father was a doctor. As a doctor, he had to take careful note of a patient's symptoms, or signs of illness, to understand what was making a patient sick. He taught Aristotle to observe people and the world around him carefully.

3. Plato taught Aristotle how important abstract ideals and knowledge are. Aristotle and Plato disagreed and argued with each other from time to time. Aristotle admired Plato greatly, but he once said, "Plato is dear to me, but dearer still is truth."

A Keen Observer

4. Aristotle also added to the knowledge of his day by collecting and examining insects, animals, and plants. He loved to study animals. He dissected more than fifty different types of animals in order to learn about them.

5. From his years of careful observation, Aristotle realized that there is always more than one way to explain things. For example, an animal could be understood by what it looked like, what it was made of, how it moved, and what it could do. All these different explanations were important and necessary.

6. Aristotle didn't know it, but by collecting facts, analyzing them, and coming up with theories about his observations, he was developing the basics of scientific research. It's true that Aristotle didn't go as far as later philosophers did in testing out his ideas.

Some of his ideas turned out to be wrong. However, he helped move philosophy down the path that would eventually lead to modern science.

7. Like other philosophers, Aristotle also wrote about what it means to lead a good and just life. He believed that the purpose of life is to exercise one's abilities and virtues reasonably. In his book *Nicomachean* (/nihk*oh*mak*ee*un/) *Ethics,* he said, "Virtue, therefore, is a kind of moderation or mean as it aims at the **mean**, or moderate amount." Aristotle meant that people should avoid extremes of all kinds. Just as they should eat neither too much nor too little, so they should avoid both evil deeds on the one hand and self-righteousness on the other. Aristotle believed that a truly virtuous person is neither cowardly nor foolishly brave. Aristotle wrote, "It is possible to feel fear, confidence, desire, anger, pity—but to feel these emotions at the right times, on the right occasions, and toward the right people in the right ways is the best course." This idea of living moderately is sometimes called "the golden mean."

8. Aristotle also examined politics, or the life of the state. He was interested in determining the best kinds of governments. He wanted to identify which types of governments care for the citizens and not just the rulers. So he inspected dozens of city-states. In his book *The Politics,* Aristotle wrote that the purpose of the state was to make "the good life" possible for its citizens. The state should create a society in which people could live nobly, honorably, and well.

A Man of His Time

9. Aristotle was a man of his time, however, and he did not believe that all people were equal. He valued men above women. He believed that aristocrats were morally superior to non-aristocrats. He also believed in slavery. He felt that an enslaved person was the property of the slave owner just as much as an animal or a tool.

10. Aristotle's influence lasted for centuries. During the European Middle Ages, he was so important that he was referred to simply as "the Philosopher."

11. The great Athenian philosophers, Socrates, Plato, and Aristotle, taught each other to use reason to examine their lives, society, and the world around them. Much of what we know and think about today is based on the principles of reason and observation that began with these philosophers of ancient Greece.

NAME: _____

DATE: _____

11.1 CONTINUED ASSESSMENT

Questions

6. PART A: What is the main text structure that the author uses in this passage?

   _____

   _____

   PART B: What evidence from the text supports your answer in Part A?

   _____

   _____

   _____

   _____

   _____

   _____

   _____

   _____

   _____

   _____

   _____

7. PART A: What sort of education did Aristotle receive?

_____

_____

PART B: What evidence from the text supports your answer in Part A?

_____

_____

_____

_____

_____

8. What does the term "golden mean" refer to?
   A. It refers to a system of classification.
   B. It refers to a method of forming theories.
   C. It refers to a political ideal.
   D. It refers to a properly balanced life.

9. What resulted from Aristotle's failure to test out his ideas?

_____

_____

_____

_____

_____

NAME: _____

DATE: _____

11.1 CONTINUED ASSESSMENT

10. What ideas of Aristotle's would most people find unacceptable today?

_____
_____
_____
_____
_____
_____
_____

11. Why is Aristotle admired today despite his flaws?

_____
_____
_____
_____
_____
_____
_____

Reading Comprehension Score: _____ *of 11 points.*

Writing Prompt: Write a short description of ancient Greek civilization that includes information from BOTH assessment passages. Use some sentences that demonstrate your understanding of properly punctuated compound sentences, correct use of conjunctions, restrictive and nonrestrictive clauses, and words with Greek and Roman roots and affixes.

Writing Prompt Score: _____ of 4 points.

NAME: _____

DATE: _____

11.1 CONTINUED — ASSESSMENT

Grammar

Complete the following sentence stems to create a compound sentence using the correct punctuation and the conjunction in parentheses.

1. (but) Rhonda's favorite sport is running _____
   _____

2. (or) I can take the bus to school _____
   _____

3. (and) Jake finished his homework _____
   _____

Correctly add a semicolon (;) between the two independent clauses in each compound sentence.

4. Yesterday it was sunny today it rained.

5. We went to the beach it was a great trip.

Read each sentence. Find the nonrestrictive clause. If it is punctuated correctly, circle "correct." If it is punctuated incorrectly, circle "incorrect."

6. My house (the blue one on the corner) is easy to find.

   correct   incorrect

7. Jaime, my best friend is a very good listener.

   correct   incorrect

8. Friday the last day of the school week—is when we leave for vacation.

   correct   incorrect

9. Did you know that Rodrigo, my friend from camp, is a great guitar player?

   correct   incorrect

10. (Sparta) an ancient Greek city-state, had very well trained soldiers.

    correct   incorrect

> Grammar Score: _____ of 10 points.

NAME (OPTIONAL): _____

DATE: _____

11.1 CONTINUED | ASSESSMENT

Morphology

Write the meaning of each Greek or Latin root, prefix, or suffix.

1. ante _____

2. astron _____

3. bios _____

4. –en (adj.) _____

5. –en (v.) _____

6. ge _____

7. mega– _____

8. micro– _____

9. mini– _____

| Morphology Score: _____ of 9 points. |
| Total Score for Unit Assessment: _____ of 34 points. |

NAME: _____

DATE: _____

11.2 ACTIVITY PAGE

Unit Feedback Survey
Unit 4: *The Heritage of Ancient Greece and Rome*

Please use a scale of 1–5, with 1 being "Not at All," 3 being "OK," and 5 being "Very Much." Circle the number that best describes your opinion. Then answer the remaining questions.

How much did you like reading the selections in *The Heritage of Ancient Greece and Rome*?

1   2   3   4   5

What, if anything, did you like about the selections that you read?

_____

_____

_____

What, if anything, did you not like about the selections that you read?

_____

_____

_____

Were you able to read and understand these selections on your own, or did you have difficulty?

_____

_____

Would you recommend this unit to your friends or other students?   YES   NO

In your opinion, how well did your teacher teach this unit?

1   2   3   4   5

What kinds of activities did you like best?

_____

_____

_____

_____

What kinds of activities did you like least?

_____

_____

_____

_____

What could your teacher have done differently in teaching the unit to improve your experience with this unit?

_____

_____

_____

_____

NAME: _____

DATE: _____

PP.1 ASSESSMENT

Mid-Unit Comprehension Check—*The Heritage of Ancient Greece and Rome*

1. The Greek city-state of Athens is known as which of these?
   A. the birthplace of freedom
   B. the birthplace of civilization
   C. the birthplace of democracy
   D. the birthplace of corruption

2. What did Athenians teach their sons to make them good debaters?
   A. rhetoric and logic
   B. ostracism and patriotism
   C. heroism and bribery
   D. citizenship and leadership

3. Which choice names the two types of law used to govern ancient Athens?
   A. oligarchy and democracy
   B. the Assembly and the Boule
   C. the *Iliad* and the *Odyssey*
   D. public and private

4. Which of these most strongly shaped the culture of ancient Sparta?
   A. the arts
   B. the military
   C. religion
   D. helots

5. How many kings ruled Sparta at any given time?

    A. one

    B. two

    C. three

    D. four

6. In ancient Greece, which word was a synonym for *Spartan*?

    A. *laconic*

    B. *aristocratic*

    C. *patriotic*

    D. *athletic*

7. Which of these emerged as the strongest member of the Delian League?

    A. Persia

    B. Sparta

    C. Dionysus

    D. Athens

8. Who is credited with bringing about the Golden Age of Athens?

    A. Aristophanes

    B. Sophocles

    C. Pericles

    D. Pheidias

9. What were the two types of dramatic performance that developed in ancient Athens?

    A. conversation and discussion

    B. comedy and tragedy

    C. conversation and comedy

    D. discussion and tragedy

NAME: _____

DATE: _____

10. How did the ancient Greeks explain the world before the development of philosophy?

    A. They used myth.

    B. They used reason.

    C. They used logic.

    D. They used phenomena.

11. Who is considered the most significant of the ancient Greek philosophers?

    A. Heraclitus

    B. Thales

    C. Socrates

    D. Anaximenes

12. What is the practice of seeking truth by asking questions called?

    A. the Socratic method

    B. the Sophist method

    C. the Platonic method

    D. the Athenian method

13. Which leader's death marked the beginning of the Hellenistic Period?

    A. Darius III

    B. King Ptolemy

    C. King Gordius

    D. Alexander the Great

14. At what point did Alexander's army decide they didn't want to fight anymore?

    A. when they reached the Mediterranean Sea

    B. when they reached western India

    C. when they reached Asia Minor

    D. when they reached Alexandria, Egypt

15. For what is Alexandria, Egypt, most remembered today?

    A. its use of attack elephants

    B. its victories over the Persian Empire

    C. its alliance with Babylon

    D. its extensive library

16. What were the two most significant city-states of ancient Greece, and what were some similarities and differences between them?

    _____

    _____

    _____

    _____

17. What were some of the distinguishing features of the Golden Age of Athens?

    _____

    _____

    _____

    _____

NAME: _____

DATE: _____

PP.1 CONTINUED — ASSESSMENT

18. What was Plato's connection to Socrates?

_____
_____
_____
_____
_____
_____
_____
_____

19. Where did Alexander the Great come from, and what was his influence on the history of Greece?

_____
_____
_____
_____
_____
_____
_____
_____

Mid-Unit Comprehension Check Score: _____ *of 19 points.*

NAME: _____

DATE: _____

PP.2 ASSESSMENT

End-of-Unit Comprehension Check—
The Heritage of Ancient Greece and Rome

1. According to legend, who founded Rome?
    A. Julius Caesar
    B. Romulus Augustulus
    C. Romulus and Remus
    D. Pompey and Crassus

2. Which of these was true of very early Rome?
    A. It was ruled by kings.
    B. It was an autocratic republic.
    C. It was ruled by plebians.
    D. It was a dictatorship.

3. Which group constituted the Roman aristocracy?
    A. plebians
    B. tribunes
    C. generals
    D. patricians

4. How did the Roman Republic treat most of the people it conquered?
    A. It enslaved them.
    B. It made them citizens.
    C. It wiped them out.
    D. It forced them to pay tribute.

5. What had changed about the Roman army by the time of Julius Caesar?
   A. It allowed plebians to serve.
   B. It had become professional.
   C. It had become poorly trained.
   D. It was run by Roman governors.

6. What happened when Julius Caesar led his army into Rome?
   A. Civil war erupted.
   B. Rome became a republic.
   C. Caesar was elected consul.
   D. Caesar became Rome's first emperor.

7. How was Julius Caesar's dictatorship different from that of earlier dictators?
   A. He stepped down after six months.
   B. He had been elected to his position by the Senate.
   C. He shared his power with two other generals.
   D. He refused to step down after six months.

8. How did the reign of Julius Caesar end?
   A. He was voted out of office.
   B. He stepped down.
   C. He was assassinated.
   D. He was arrested and imprisoned.

9. Who was the first Christian Emperor of Rome?
   A. Nero
   B. Augustus
   C. Diocletian
   D. Constantine

NAME: _____
DATE: _____

PP.2 ASSESSMENT
CONTINUED

10. How had the Roman economy changed by 200 CE, and what resulted from those changes?

   _____

   _____

   _____

   _____

   _____

11. How did Emperors Diocletian and Constantine try to strengthen Rome's economy?

   _____

   _____

   _____

   _____

   _____

12. How did Rome's government change as the empire declined?

   _____

   _____

   _____

   _____

   _____

13. What was the Byzantine Empire?

_____

_____

_____

_____

_____

14. How long did the Roman and Byzantine Empires last, and what brought about their fall?

_____

_____

_____

_____

_____

End-of-Unit Comprehension Check Score: _____ of 14 points.

NAME: _____

DATE: _____

PP.3 ASSESSMENT

Grammar: Punctuation in Compound Sentences

The following compound sentences are incorrect. Rewrite each sentence with the correct punctuation.

1. I lost my notebook but I found it later.

   _____

   _____

2. Raina and Selena will go to the park before lunch or they will go later.

   _____

   _____

3. Rondo is the top student in math he is also very good at English.

   _____

   _____

4. I will meet Avery at the library and we will study for our test.

   _____

   _____

5. Is Shawna going to the dance or is she playing basketball tonight?

   _____

   _____

6. I'm in the drama club my brother Luis is in the band.

   _____

   _____

7. The old building has a hole in its roof and it is leaking.

   _____

   _____

8. Do you want pepperoni pizza or do you prefer mushroom?

   _____

   _____

NAME: _____

DATE: _____

PP.4 ASSESSMENT

Grammar: Punctuation with Nonrestrictive Clauses

The following sentences contain nonrestrictive clauses but don't include any punctuation. Find the nonrestrictive clause in each sentence. Then rewrite the sentence using commas, dashes, or parentheses around the nonrestrictive clause.

1. The box of crackers which doesn't cost a lot at the grocery store was twice as expensive at Convenience Mart.

   _____

   _____

2. Tiffany who hates rainy weather got caught in a thundershower without her umbrella.

   _____

   _____

3. That kitten the one with the black spots is the cutest.

   _____

   _____

4. The road race which occurs every year will take place the day after Thanksgiving.

   _____

   _____

5. Marcus a really funny guy I know made me laugh so hard that my sides hurt.

   _____

   _____

6. The identical twins Ellie and Lynne are difficult to tell apart.

   _____

   _____

7. The ocean which is a shade of blue-green looks beautiful in the sunlight.

   _____

   _____

NAME: _____
DATE: _____

PP.5 ASSESSMENT

Morphology: Roots *ante, astron, bios, ge*

Use what you know about roots ante, astron, bios, *and* ge *to complete each sentence so that it shows the meaning of the underlined word. If you are not sure of the meaning, check your answer in a dictionary.*

1. Mark is an astronomer who _____.

   _____

   _____

2. In my biology class, _____.

   _____

   _____

3. We used a geographic map to _____.

   _____

   _____

4. A biohazard is dangerous to _____.

   _____

   _____

5. An astronomic price is _____.

   _____

   _____

6. The geologist was interested _____.

_____

_____

7. A geophysicist studies the physics of _____.

_____

_____

8. The astronauts _____.

_____

_____

NAME: _____
DATE: _____

PP.6 RESOURCE

Morphology: Prefixes *mega–*, *mini–*, *micro–*; Suffix *–en*

Use what you know about prefixes mega–, mini–, micro– *and suffix* –en *to complete each sentence so that it shows the meaning of the underlined word. If you are not sure of the meaning, check your answer in a dictionary.*

1. The scientist used a microscope to _____
   _____.

2. The minuscule amount of rain _____
   _____.

3. Microbes are living things _____
   _____.

4. The roller coaster has a minimum height requirement of 50 inches for passengers, so
   _____
   _____.

5. You can lighten the load in your backpack by _____
   _____.

Core Knowledge Language Arts | Grade 6   Activity Book | Unit 3   **115**

6. If you speak into a megaphone, _____

_____

_____.

7. The woolen sweater is _____

_____

_____.

8. The song was a megahit because _____

_____

_____.

NAME:
DATE:

SR.1 RESOURCE

Student Resources

In this section you will find:

- SR.1—Glossary

- SR.2—Writing Process Diagram

- SR.3—Proofreading Symbols

- SR.4—Individual Code Chart

NAME: _____

DATE: _____

SR.1 RESOURCE

Glossary for *The Heritage of Ancient Greece and Rome*

A

adequate, *adj.* enough to meet a need

adversity, *n.* hardship or misfortune

alliance, *n.* a group of city-states (or countries or people) who agree to help one another

ambitious, *adj.* wanting to succeed

architecture, *n.* the art of designing and constructing buildings

arrogant, *adj.* having a pushy, snobbish attitude

B

barbarian, *n.* a person, often foreign, considered inferior and violent (**barbarians**)

betrayal, *n.* the act of violating a friendship

biased, *adj.* unfair toward a person, group, or viewpoint

bribery, *n.* the act of giving money or something of value to illegally influence a person in power

C

campaign, *n.* a military operation intended to achieve a particular objective (**campaigns**)

career, *n.* a job

chaos, *n.* a state of complete confusion

charming, *adj.* pleasant, attractive, likable

civilization, *n.* a society, or group of people, with similar religious beliefs, customs, language, and government (**civilizations**)

complex, *n.* a group of similar buildings; *adj.* having many connected parts

contemporary, *adj.* existing at the same time

contradiction, *n.* the state when two things oppose one another (**contradictions**)

convulsion, *n.* a violent, unwilling muscle contraction

council, *n.* a group of people who meet regularly to make decisions

D

debate, *v.* to formally discuss or argue multiple views about a topic

declare, *v.* to state something as a truth (**declaring**)

disciplined, *adj.* self-controlled

disorganized, *adj.* not under sufficient control

distinction, *n.* category or grouping

E

emphasize, *v.* to stress strongly, give special importance to (**emphasized**)

excel, *v.* to be very good at knowing or doing something

excerpt, *n.* a short piece from a larger body of work

extraordinary, *adj.* unusual and amazing

extravagant, *adj.* more than necessary, excessive

F

fateful, *adj.* having significant and negative results

found, *v.* to establish or build (**founded**)

fresco, *n.* a watercolor painting on plaster

frieze, *n.* a wide, sculpted wall decoration

G

grandeur, *n.* the state of being remarkable, very impressive, or special

groundbreaking, *adj.* never done before

H

hemlock, *n.* a highly poisonous plant

hostile, *adj.* unfriendly toward someone or something, in opposition to

I

influence, *v.* to have an effect on (**influenced**)

influential, *adj.* having a great deal of control

inherit, *v.* to receive something from a former owner or someone who came before (**inherited**)

L

legend, *n.* a story that has been handed down from person to person over a long period of time; the story may or may not be true

M

mislead, *v.* to purposefully cause someone to form a wrong idea (**misled**)

misleading, *adj.* tending to cause people to believe the wrong thing

modest, *adj.* small or limited

P

papyrus, *n.* in ancient times, a material used to write on

professional, *adj.* done as a career or profession

proposal, *n.* an idea or plan put forward for discussion with others

prosperity, *n.* the state of being materially successful

public figure, *n.* someone the public in general knows about

R

raucous, *adj.* wild and noisy

recruit, *v.* to obtain the services of (**recruited**)

revolt, *n.* an attempt to put an end to a ruling power

rite, *n.* a ceremony, usually religious (**rites**)

rivalry, *n.* a competition between groups for the same goals

S

shortcoming, *n.* a fault in someone's personality or character (**shortcomings**)

station, *v.* to place someone or something, especially military, in a certain place (**stationed**)

status, *n.* position in society

stronghold, *n.* a strong, secure shelter

successor, *n.* a person or thing that follows another person or thing

NAME:

DATE:

T

term, *n.* a set amount of time that a person spends in a certain position in a government.

tirelessly, *adv.* with a lot of effort and energy

U

unified, *adj.* whole, united, acting as one

unity, *n.* the state of being whole or in agreement

urgency, *n.* a state of extreme importance

urn, *n.* a ceramic vase that has a base (**urns**)

V

victorious, *adj.* having won a fight or battle

W

wrong, *n.* an illegal action (**wrongs**)

NAME:
DATE:

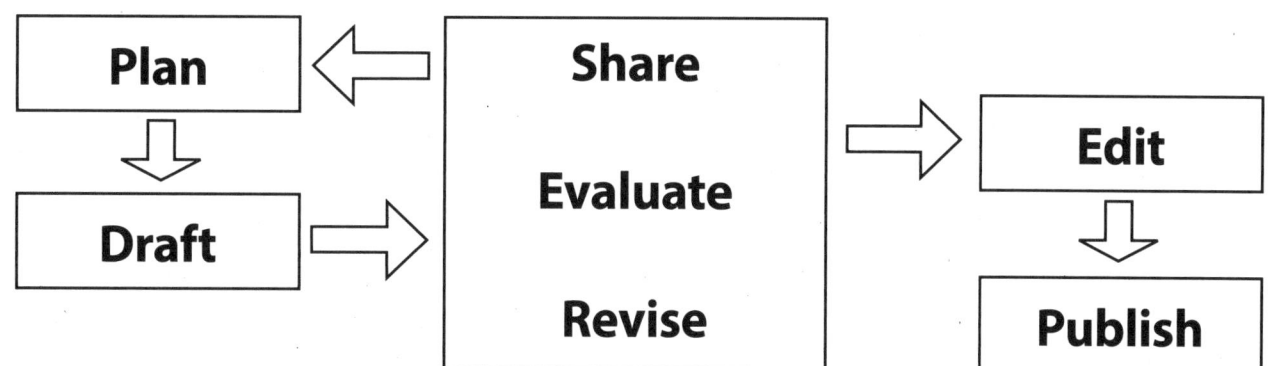

NAME: _____
DATE: _____

SR.3 RESOURCE

Proofreading Symbols

∧	Insert
⊙	Insert period
∧,	Insert comma
∨'	Insert apostrophe
#	Insert space
¶	New paragraph
no ¶	No new paragraph
⌒	Close up the space
b̳ cap	Capitalize
B̸ lc	Make lowercase (small letter)
ℓ	Delete
rwd.	Reword
←	Move according to arrow direction
r̃e͠tr	Transpose
[	Move to the left
]	Move to the right
⩓a	Add a letter

Core Knowledge Language Arts | Grade 6   Activity Book | Unit 3   **125**

NAME: _____

DATE: _____

SR.4 RESOURCE

Individual Code Chart

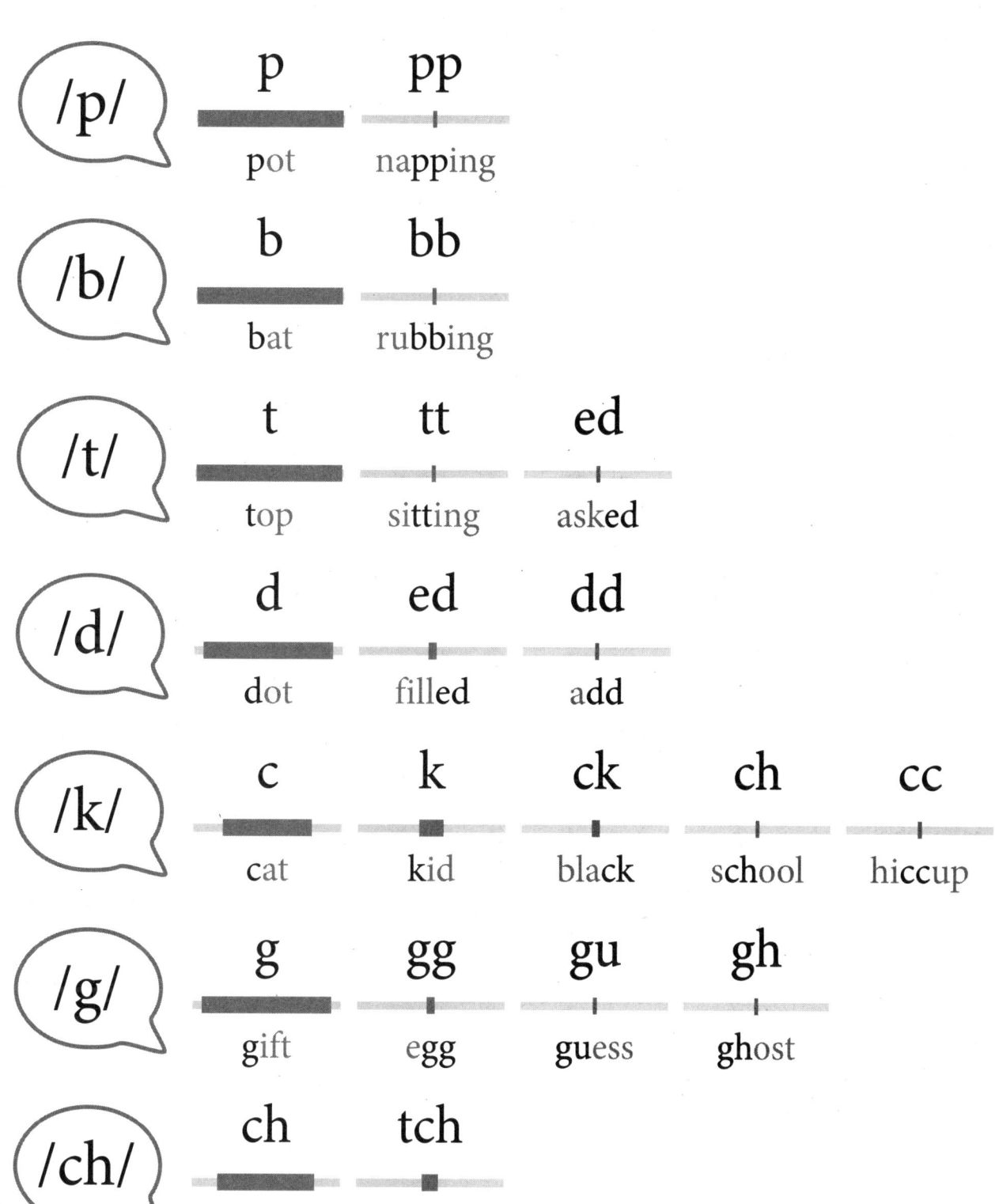

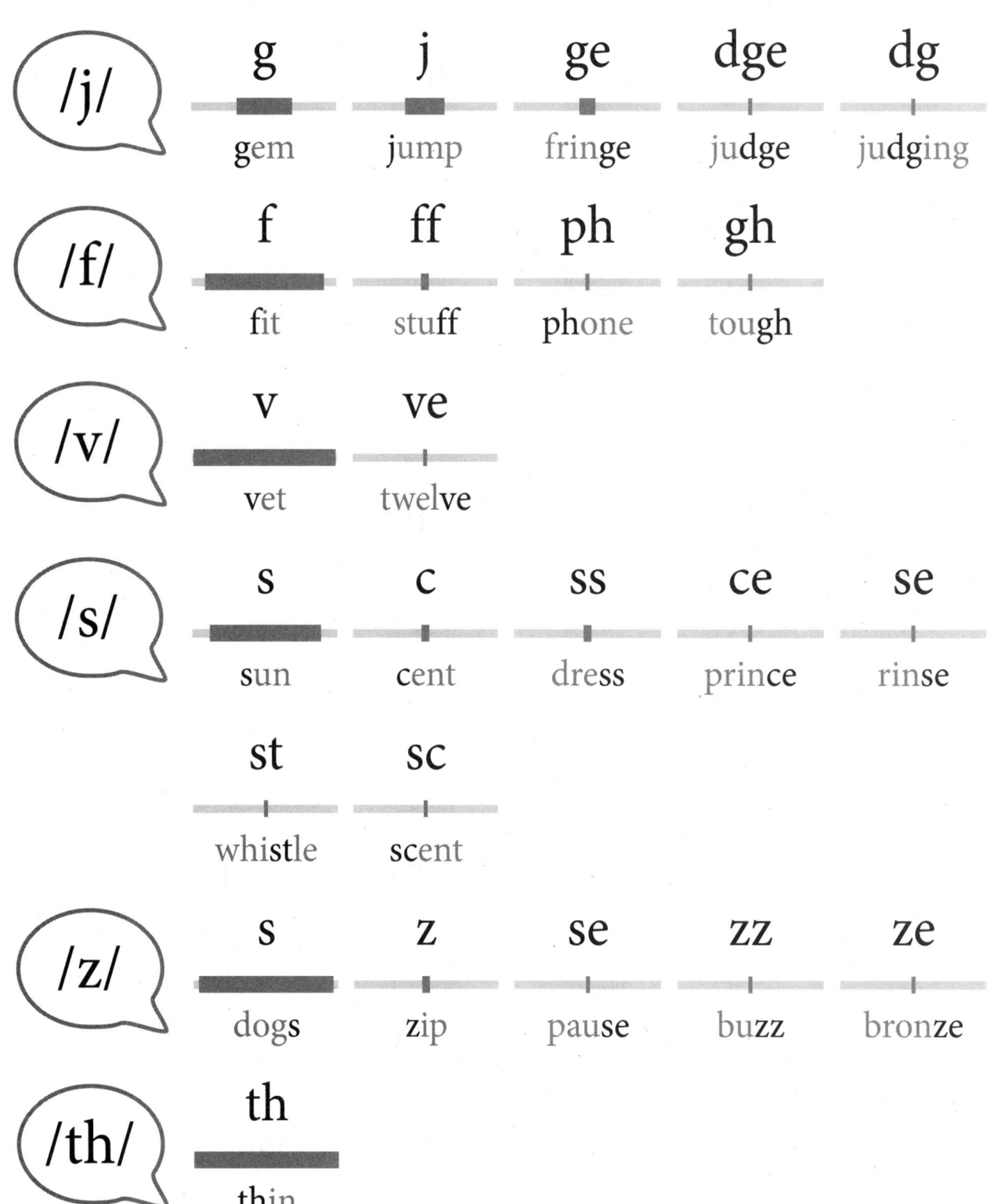

NAME: _____
DATE: _____

SR.4 CONTINUED RESOURCE

/th/ — **th** — them

/m/ — **m** mad — **mm** swimming — **mb** thumb

/n/ — **n** nut — **nn** running — **kn** knock — **gn** sign

/ng/ — **ng** sing — **n** pink

/r/ — **r** red — **rr** ferret — **wr** wrist

/l/ — **l** lip — **ll** bell

/h/ — **h** hot

Core Knowledge Language Arts | Grade 6   Activity Book | Unit 3   129

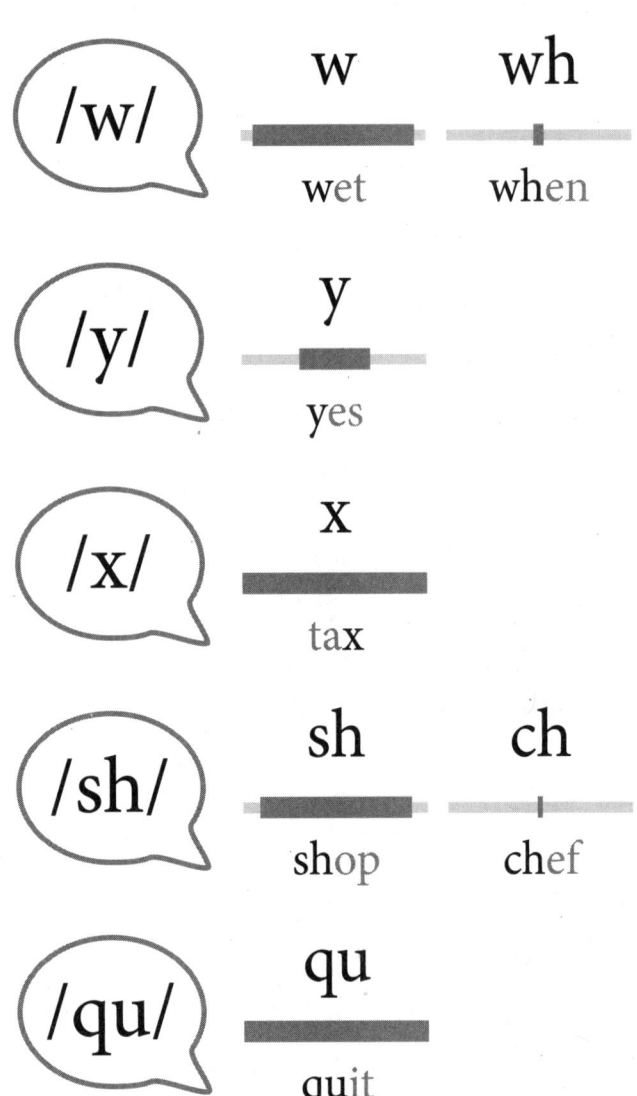

NAME:
DATE:

SR.4 RESOURCE CONTINUED

/a/ — a (hat)

/i/ — i (it), y (myth)

/e/ — e (pet), ea (head)

/u/ — u (but), o (son), o_e (come), ou (touch)

/o/ — o (hop), a (lava)

/ə/ — a (about), e (debate)

/ə/ + /l/ — al (animal), le (apple), el (travel), ul (awful), il (pencil)

Core Knowledge Language Arts | Grade 6   Activity Book | Unit 3   131

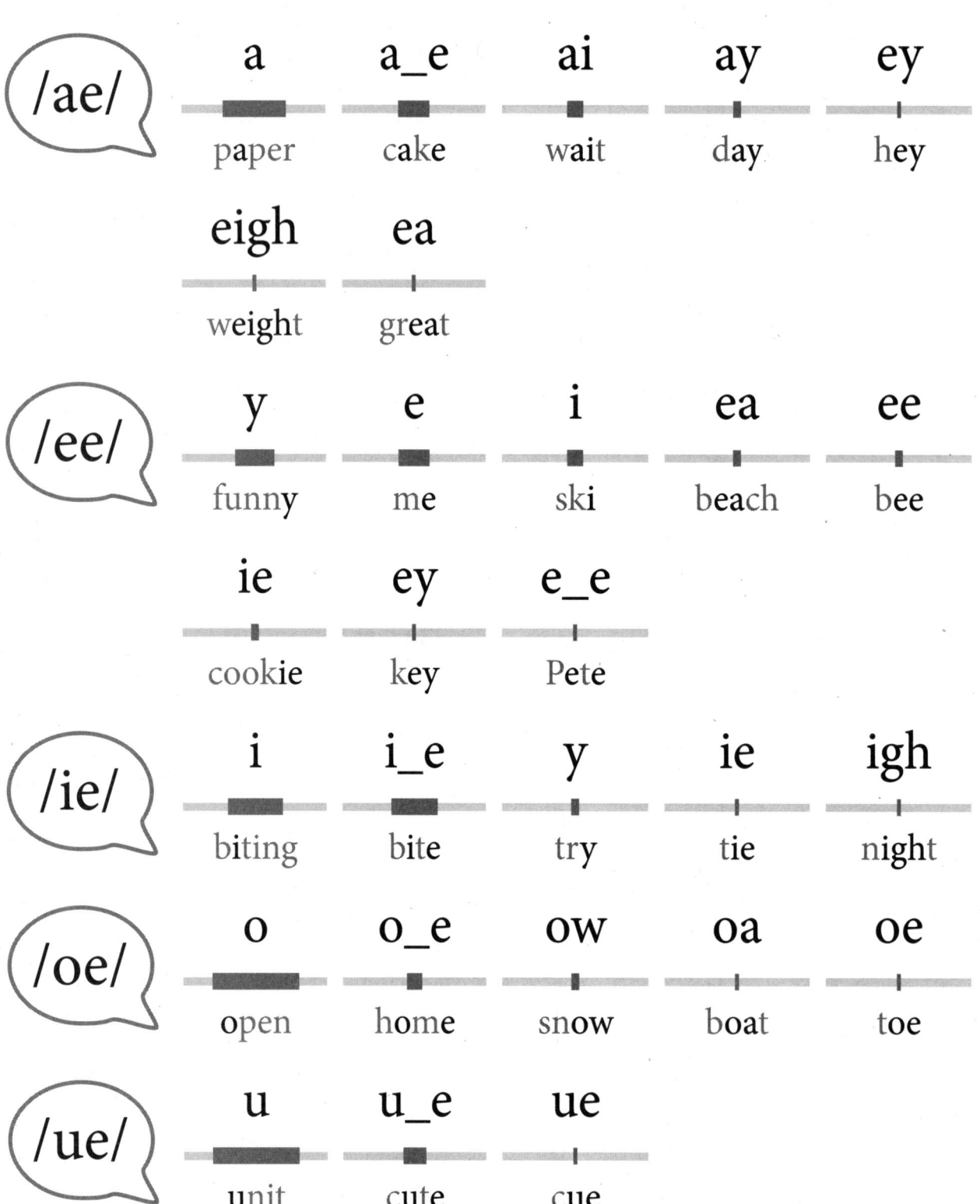

NAME: _____
DATE: _____

SR.4 CONTINUED — RESOURCE

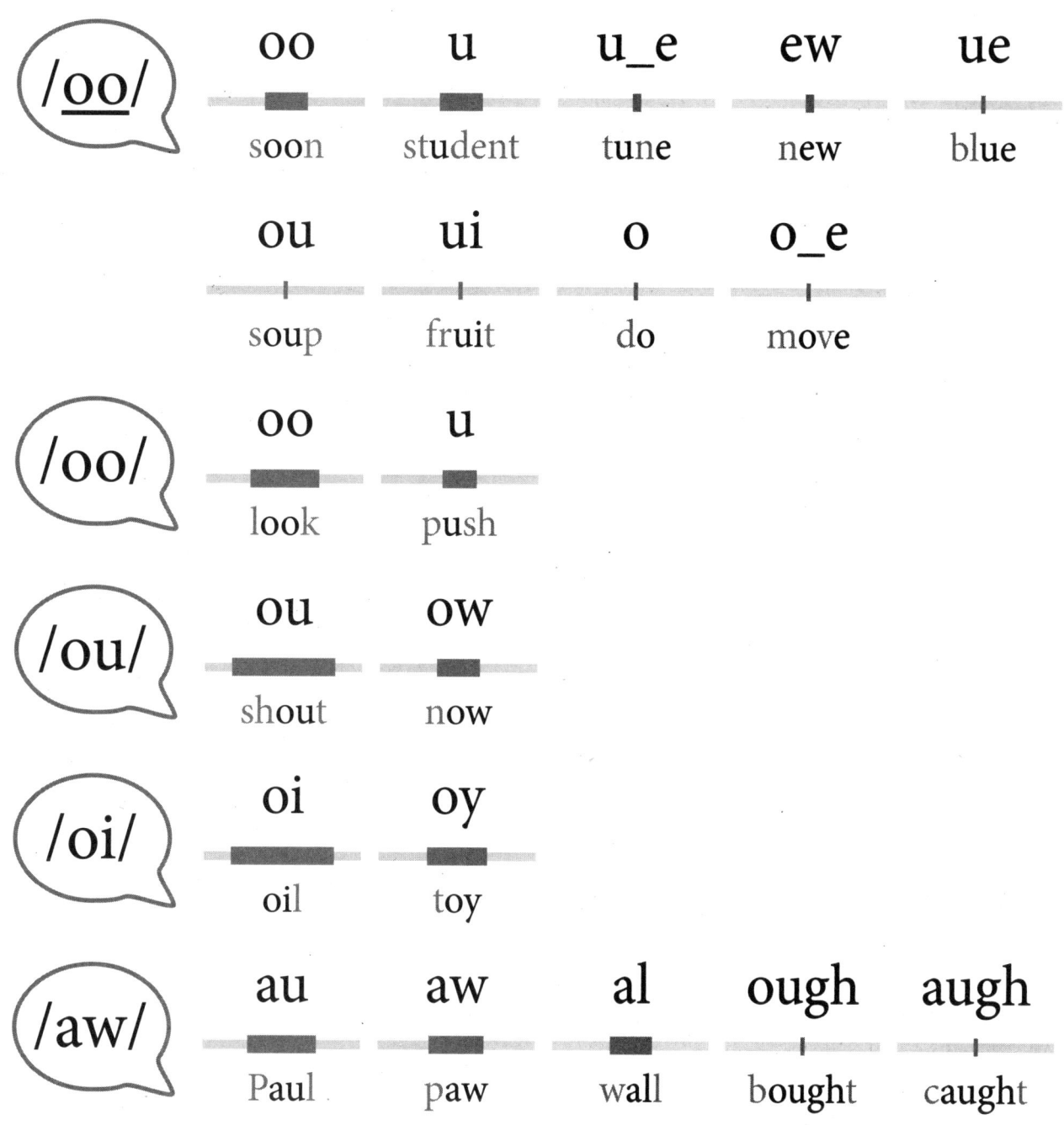

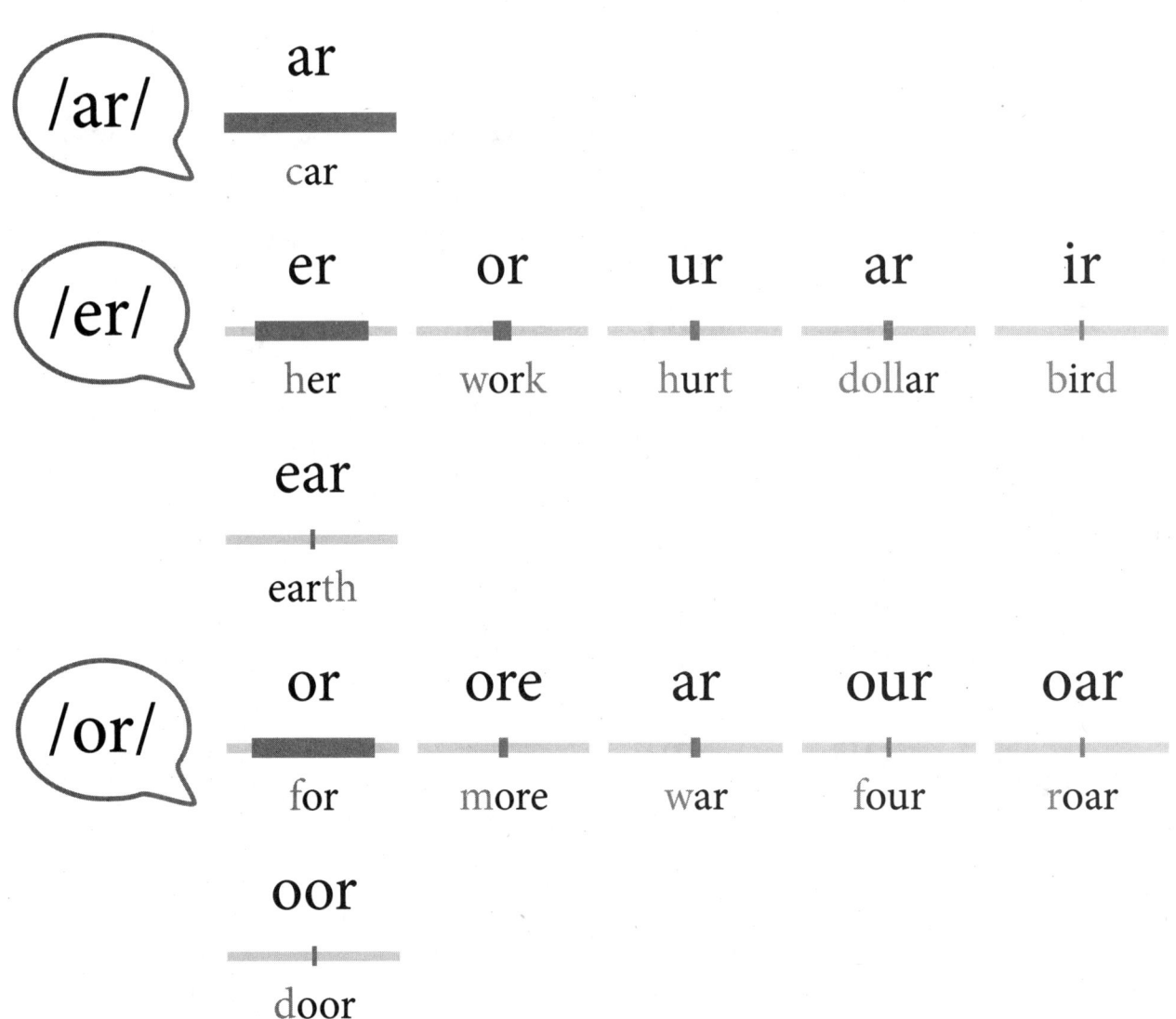

Core Knowledge Language Arts®

President
Linda Bevilacqua

Editorial Staff
Sally Guarino
Sue Herndon

Illustration and Photo Credits
Ivan Pesic: Cover, i, 1

Subject Matter Expert
Michael J. Carter, Ph.d., Brock University, Classics Department